1952

A YEAR TO REMEMBER

1952

A YEAR TO REMEMBER

by
Richard Hease

in association with
British Pathe News
and
Dennis Fairey and Associates

A Year to Remember -1952

First Published in book form in Great Britain by Mistral Publishing Ltd. 1991 in association with British Pathe News Ltd.

Copyright Mistral Publishing Ltd. 1991 and Richard Hease, Academy House, 56-58 Crewys Road, London NW2 2AD.

ISBN - 1 874053 10 3

A CIP catalogue record for this book is available from the British Library.

Printed and bound by Waterside Press, Hatfield, England.

Design and Typesetting by Dennis Fairey & Associates Ltd., Chiltern House, 184 High Street, Berkhamsted, Herts HP4 3AP

Mistral
PUBLISHING

1952

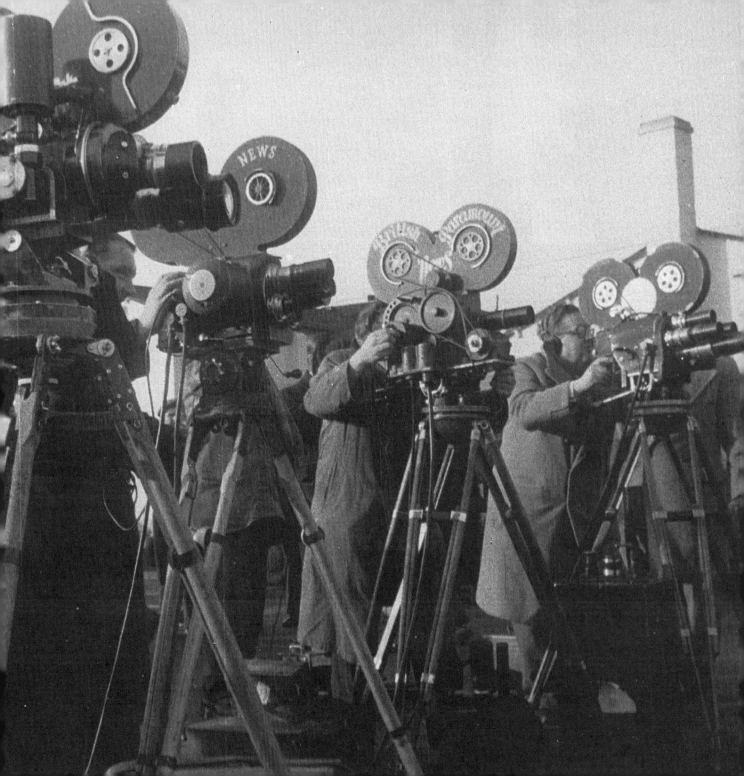

Pathe Review

We are all a part of history wherever we are and whatever we are doing. World events shape our memories and for most of the 20th Century those events were filmed and explained by Pathe. Pathe News captured history in motion, creating a living chronicle of a turbulent century.

The following pages contain actual pictures taken from the Pathe newsreels accompanied by the slightly edited version of the original transcripts which became a very distinctive style over the years.

The World in 1952

1952 was a year characterised by conflict and technology. Technology played an important part in the emerging world order as atomic weapons dominated super power thinking. In 1945 America had used two such devices on Japan to end the war in the Pacific. For a time the United States believed it had the monopoly of such weapons and set itself up as guardian of freedom under the shield of the atomic bomb.

In 1949 the Soviet Union successfully tested its own weapon. The balance of terror began. By 1952 Britain had decided to enter the atomic club and tested its first device at Monte Bello to the North West of Australia, but the Americans had gone one stage further. Atomic bombs gave way to thermo-nuclear weapons in the form of the hydrogen bomb. The United States tested its first H-bomb at Eniwetok Atoll in 1952 and the force of the explosion vapourised the whole island.

**The Scottish soldiers of
'Black Watch' arrive
in Korea.**

In Asia the Korean war continued. In 1950 the Communist forces of North Korea had broken through the 38th parallel, the internationally agreed border between North and South. The Americans went to the aid of their Southern Allies and soon a UN force, with a large British contingent, had fought the Communists back towards the Chinese border.

China, which had only just become a Communist State under Mao Tse-tung, decided to assist their Korean comrades and invaded the country, pushing the UN forces back again.

1951 produced a stalemate between the two sides. An uneasy peace lasted for a time but fighting broke out again as the situation became more and more frustrating.

In 1952 the UN side undertook heavy bombing raids against key installations and cities in the Northern sector. In Indo-China, an area covering modern Vietnam, Cambodia and Laos, the French fought Viet Minh rebels in the area known as North Vietnam. Led by Ho Chi Minh and General Giap, the Communists caused much harm to the French Colonial presence. The French attempted to smash the Viet Minh but without much success.

In the West there were fears that the Chinese might intervene and broaden the Asian conflict. America considered fighting on the side of the French but was dissuaded by Britain's unwillingness to help. America's interest in the region increased over the next decade and by 1965 the Vietnam War had begun.

Elsewhere in the world trouble was brewing in Britain's Colonial terittories. In Kenya, the Mau Mau, led by Jomo Kenyatta, launched a terrorist campaign against white farmers. British troops attempted to put down the rebellion.

In Egypt the corrupt regime of King Farouk was toppled by a military coup run by General Neguib. In Cairo and around the canal zone in Suez rioting claimed 17 British lives. Anti-British feelings were running high and the future of Britain's presence in the country and around the Suez Canal was being called into question.

Within four years a full political crisis was to shake the British Government severely.

**Political unrest as army tanks
dominate the streets of Cairo.**

MR. CHURCHILL IN AMERICA

January

As the 'Queen Mary' approached New York, the US Coastguard Cutter 'Nav-E-Sink', flying a White Ensign, rushed Mr Churchill and party to Brooklyn to make up lost time. Delayed by her anchor jamming, the 'Queen Mary' was 30 hours late according to schedule and the Premier had an urgent lunch date with the President in Washington. He landed at Brooklyn Pier with daughter Sarah and was greeted by Mayor Impelleteri of New York.

At Floyd Bennett Naval Air Station, Mr Churchill boarded the President's personal aircraft, 'Independence'. Mr Eden and 10 other delegates accompanied him for talks which covered a large number of subjects, including Britain's problems, Western defence and also the atom bomb.

A little over an hour later 'Independence' landed at Washington and America saluted the President's distinguished visitor. As he landed Mr Churchill was welcomed by Mr Truman. Though no immediate sensational results were expected, this British-American get -together was to have strengthened the bonds between the two great countries.

RECORD SNOWS IN CALIFORNIA

January 1952

Night and day, snow ploughs attempted to clear California's worst blizzards in 50 years.

In some areas, cars were buried up to 10 feet deep in the snow. At Donner Pass the snow was 26 feet deep along the highway.

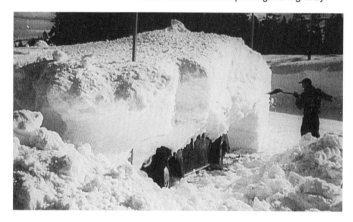

Digging went on for hours to free the trapped 'City of San Francisco' from snow up to 26 feet deep.

Trapped by the blizzards, the crack streamliner 'City of San Francisco' from Chicago was snowbound, although her 200 passengers were taken off by rescue squads. After long hours of digging she became free at last and five days behind schedule the luxury train resumed her journey to the coast and a much warmer climate.

IKE WINS

July 1952

In Chicago's Convention Hall the most frantic Republican Convention in years headed towards its climax. As candidates' names were raised in nomination, Senator Dirksen offered Taft's name to the gathering saying...

"I place before you for your prayerful and earnest consideration Mr Integrity, Mr Republican, Mr American...my friend Bob Taft".

Then Eisenhower was nominated by Maryland's Governor McKeldin saying...

"I am proud to place before this Convention the name of Dwight Eisenhower".

Then the most dramatic part of the long and bitter convention began as the balloting on nominees commenced, state by state.

As balloting ended Ike lacked nine votes but Minnesota changed its vote, making the sensational statement...

"...the Chair of Minnesota wishes to change its vote to Eisenhower"

That was enough to win a first ballot victory for Ike. At the suggestion of Taft and Warren leaders Chairman Martin said...

"...that the nomination of Dwight Eisenhower be signified. All those in favour say aye..."

"aye" was the resounding response.

" It's a vote; therefore General Eisenhower is hereby nominated to be the Republican Party's official candidate for Presidential elections."

KOREAN RAID ON RED CAPITAL

August 1952

These pictures represent the first films of the United Nations 24-hour air attack on Pyongyang, the red capital in North Korea.

Flak appeared from more than100 gun positions below as B29s approached their target, passing over territory already hit by fighter bombers. It was part of a determined drive to prevent enemy build-ups during the truce talks.

Air units from five United Nations countries participated in an all-out blow at enemy installations above the 38th parallel.

B29 Bombers attack to prevent large-scale enemy offensive.

EYGPTIAN COUP D'ETAT

August 1952

From Cairo came this first authentic picture of the bloodless coup by which the army took over control of Egypt.

It was the end of the King's attempt to maintain power. Troops in the street were the first indication of the change to most people until the broadcasting station was seized, and it was announced that General Neguib, the Commander in Chief (whom Farouk refused as War Minister) had taken control and the army were ordered to guard strategic points. The declared aim was to stop corruption.

They struck at the top and General Neguib displayed the abdication papers signed by King Farouk in favour of his seven months-old son. At the Ras el Tin Palace the leader of the coup was with Ali Maher, the new Premier, who secured Farouk's signature. Meanwhile from Alexandria, the Royal yacht 'Mahroussa' sailed with the ex-King and infant King for Capri.

To the ordinary Egyptian the change was greeted with some enthusiasm, so Mohamed Neguib was assured of support back home.

Since having reached the lovely island of Capri, the ex-King nursed the new King Fuad II as Queen Narriman watched. With the Royal family were Farouk's three daughters by his former marriage, Fawzia, Ferian and Fadia.

The ex-King dreamt of former glory.

FUNERAL OF EVA PERON

August 1952

The body of Eva Peron, wife of the Argentine dictator, was carried through the streets of Buenos Aires. Despite the pouring rain and bitterly cold winds, thousands waited for more than 12 hours for the procession, which included a float bearing replicas of Madam Peron's hands.

Columns of workers drew the catafalque to the headquarters of the General Labour Confederation. Here in a special chapel, Eva Peron's body was laid to rest where a huge mausoleum was to be built in her memory by public subscription.

In Buenos Aires hundreds of thousands wait to pay their last personal tributes to 30-year-old Eva Peron, the farm girl who, in nine years, rose from Movie Extra to be the most powerful woman in the Western world as wife of Argentine dictator Juan Peron.

PRESIDENT EISENHOWER

The battle for the Presidency of the United States drew to its climax while tension grew in rival camps. At his headquarters, Dwight Eisenhower, the Republican candidate, made his way on to the platform to the acclaim of his supporters as the news came in from 48 states that he was in the lead.

Earlier in the day, President Truman recorded his vote for Governor Stevenson, the Democrat candidate. He was pulling no punches in his attacks on Eisenhower but Ike looked reasonably confident of victory.

Over in Illinois, Stevenson's own state, Ike's opponent looked far from gloomy as he went to the polls, but at the Stevenson headquarters they weren't so happy because Eisenhower was steadily forging ahead, ending Stevenson's term in office.

Electric signs flashed the news "Ikes in!" Bedlam broke out among Republican supporters but it was a very different picture at Stevenson's H.Q.

"The people have made their choice and I congratulate you", was part of the telegram message that Stevenson sent to General Eisenhower.

When asked by a reporter about running for Presidency in 1956, Stevenson commented with a good-natured reply...

"1956! Examine that man's head".

The President replied to the telegram thanking Stevenson for his courteous and generous message,

"Recognising the intensity of the difficulties that lie ahead it is clearly necessary that men and women of goodwill of both parties forget the political strife through which we have passed and devote themselves to the single purpose of a better future. This I believe they will do".

Dwight D. Eisenhower became President by the greatest popular vote ever given to a White House candidate. The American people had shown their confidence in Eisenhower, followed by Britain who believed he would not fail in his tremendous task ahead.

Britain in 1952

Britain announced a new Conservative Government. In 1951 the Tories had beaten Labour at the polls but, at the beginning of 1952, it was clear that they were not planning to dismantle the Welfare State. The emergence of a distinct political consensus between the major parties resulted in the foundation of a Welfare State such as the National Health Service, and public ownership of major utilities seemed a foregone conclusion.

Britain was still suffering the hardships of rationing and shortage but, under the new government, controls were easing and life improved steadily.

1952 marked the death of George VI, a reserved but popular monarch. The nation mourned as the world witnessed the pomp and subdued ceremony of a State funeral while Princess Elizabeth, now the young Queen, became the centre of attention for the world's press.

BRITAIN EXPLODES ATOM BOMB

December 1952

These first dramatic pictures show the explosion of Britain's atomic bomb on Monte Bello island off North West Australia.

The Monte Bello islands are situated far beyond normal shipping routes and, until 1952, only pearl fishing boats entered the blue waters that lapped the cliffs surrounding their shores. Barren infertile rocks, buffeted by winds blowing in from the ocean, scorched by a dazzling sun that beat upon her empty beaches, this was the place chosen to explode Britain's first atomic weapon.

Out at sea on board the Campania, Dr Penney and his team made final adjustments to their instruments in the control laboratory. One minute to go; slowly the seconds ticked away. Suddenly thousands of tons of water, mud and sand blackened the gigantic fireball. Like a huge boiling cauldron, the mushroom-shaped cloud billowed upwards to a height of 10,000 feet within two minutes.

Rear Admiral Tourness, who was in command of the operation, and Dr Penney turned to watch the great cloud after its initial blinding flash was over. Somewhere out at sea the ship carrying the weapon had been vapourised. Smoke rose higher and higher, the strong wind twisting and sprawling it until it became a mile wide at its centre and about two and a half miles high.

To Dr Penney and his team great credit was due for this mighty British achievement. The spectacular success of the operation furthered their hopes of peace, for it seemed that by the possession of such a deadly weapon, second only to the hydrogen bomb, peace could be maintained in a troubled world.

Dr Penney.

On board the 'Campania' the crew watch as the mushroom-shaped cloud billows upwards to a height of two and a half miles.

Frantic shoppers rush through the doors for a chance to find the best bargains.

NEW YEAR BARGAINS

"They're here again, the Sales and the queues", and in those days you couldn't afford to miss a good bargain. Some people queued all night and received a welcome surprise in the form of an early morning 'cuppa' to warm them up for the battle ahead.

When the doors opened the crowds rushed in, all at once, anxious to find the bargains that tempted them in the windows. Wherever you queued there were bargains. By this time the Grand National bargain chase was well under way, as more and more frantic shoppers passed through the doors joining the early birds busily worming away.

They were like a hive of busy little bees which was enough to gladden the heart of any manager. Most buyers looked for good useful things, as they tried to avoid any flashy temptations going to their heads. You could get almost anything at these Sales except the pound out of the till. Some bargains were for the more flighty-minded, such as a sequined dress marked down from £25 to a modest £5. And to go with it a 'lovely' skunk coat slashed from £50 to £3 - what a bargain!

Reports reflected good business everywhere; with so many bargains there was no doubt that it would be a sell-out by closing time. And when the store manager was asked for his comments, he replied;

"Oh, we've had a wonderful day, sold everything - paper, string and bags".

**The 12-day attempt
to stop the freighter
'Enterprise' from
sinking ends.**

THE GALLANT 'ENTERPRISE'

January 1952

PATHE PRESENTS THE LAST MOMENTS OF THE DRAMA OF THE 'FLYING ENTERPRISE', THE END OF A SEA SAGA THAT HELD THE WORLD ENTHRALLED

Captain Carlsen, rescued from the 'Enterprise'.

Heading for the Prince of Wales Pier, the cutter 'Portwey' brought Captain Carlsen and mate Ken Dancey to a heroes' welcome from Falmouth. Overnight they had slept on the tug 'Turmoil' which picked them up when 'Flying Enterprise' was nearing her end.

Success seemed to be assured when the 'Flying Enterprise' reached within 30 miles of Falmouth. Though listing badly with her port deck awash, she still trailed slowly behind 'Turmoil' and was no worse after 300 miles of towing. The 5-inch tow-cable was holding but, to make doubly sure, they were preparing a second, until the weather broke and the calm sea gave way to gale force winds and mountainous waves. Along the shore crowds watched anxiously for sign of the little convoy but disaster loomed, as the cable snapped and 'Flying Enterprise' lay at the mercy of the gale.

Though swept off their feet by almost every wave for a day and a night and into the second day, Carlsen and Dancey tried to make fast another line from 'Turmoil' but to no avail; the battle was lost. Somehow, they had to leave the ship and the naval helicopter from Culdrose, sent to take off the two men, was forced back by the storm. Now only seamanship could save them. The 'Flying Enterprise' keeled right over on her side and the little craft raced through a heavy sea to save the two men who had to jump now or go down with the ship.

Dan Parker took in 'Turmoil' as closely as he dared as Carlsen and Dancey began to walk along the funnel. Nine minutes later they were safely on board the 'Turmoil' just as the sea poured down the funnel where they had walked only minutes before.

The doom of 'Flying Enterprise' was sealed. As she began her last plunge the sea boiled and the little rescue craft bobbed madly, the bows of the stricken ship lifted as if to say farewell. Captain Carlsen watched sadly from 'Turmoil' as across the waters came the last salute of the little ships.

Captain Carlsen's story, of how after such an ordeal he left the ship he had served so faithfully and well, had the toast of his rescuers,

"....so we decided between the two of us to walk out on the smoke stack, which we did, and with our life jackets on we jumped from the smoke stack into the sea and swam towards the tugboat 'Turmoil' where the crew was ready to pick us up. In less then nine minutes we were on board the 'Turmoil', where we were handed some warm tea and rum, some warm clothes and then we had a very welcome rest."

THE ROYAL DEPARTURE

February 1952

The King and Queen accompanied their daughter and her husband to London Airport to begin the first stage of their 30,000 mile journey to Australia and New Zealand. Princess Elizabeth and the Duke had taken the place of Their Majesties who were originally to have made the tour.

East Africa was to be their first stop, flying on the BOAC 'Argonaut Atlanta', specially converted for the journey.

It was good to see His Majesty looking so well and with 10 minutes before take-off time Their Majesties boarded 'Atlanta', to make their private farewells to the Princess and Duke.

Over the previous few months, Their Royal Highnesses had logged plenty of flying time. Princess Elizabeth had already visited Africa and America and was due to visit Asia on arrival in Ceylon; by the end of the tour she would have seen something of all five continents.

The King and Queen watched as she began her 24-hour flight to Nairobi as Britain and the Empire wished them 'Bon Voyage and happy landing'.

The King and Queen wave goodbye to their daughter as she leaves for Kenya.

SPEAKMAN VC COMES HOME

February 1952

Arriving 24 hours late from Korea, Private Bill Speakman VC, Kings Own Scottish Borderers, landed at RAF Lyneham.

Private Speakman VC comes home to a heroes' welcome.

On the left of his tunic was the much-acclaimed red ribbon. Bill, who was later to be decorated by the King at an official ceremony, received the welcome of the Mayor of Altrincham. The army sent Bill home because they didn't want to lose him. At Hill 217 he proved himself a born leader.

It was a big day in Cheshire to welcome the local boy. In Moss Lane, Altrincham, neighbours helped to prepare Bill's home for his arrival and 5,000 school children had a day off to cheer their own hero. It was a great day for Bill but he had one message for all;

"Don't forget the boys in Korea; they're doing a tough job and they're doing it well".

"...There's not very much I really can say to you all; words will not express my feelings for the way you have treated me today but there is one thing I can say: it's good to be back and thanks a lot".

But to Private Bill Speakman home meant Moss Lane, the neighbours and, above all, mum.

The army had big plans for Bill's future; they needed leaders like Private Speakman VC to shape conscripts for the future.

THE KING
DEAD
EVENING
NEWS

BRITAIN MOURNS

February 1952

Britain mourned the passing of a Monarch whose life was an inspiration to all he ruled.

The day prior to his death he was at Sandringham, King of England and the Empire but to his followers the Squire, the kindly man who passed among them until the news;

.."This is London; it is with the greatest sorrow that we have to make the following announcement...

It is announced from Sandringham at 10.45 today, February 6th 1952, that the King who retired to rest last night in his usual health passed peacefully away in his sleep early this morning".

The heart of the nation stopped. Flags lowered in tribute round the country and over the Mother of Parliaments, high over Big Ben in the capital, as the news spread - the King was dead.

Fifteen years earlier, following the abdication of his brother, George VI became King and was crowned at Westminster. With the pomp and ritual born of a thousand years, the man who had sought the quieter part in life was crowned ruler of the greatest empire in history. The Coronation oath he vowed that day he was to redeem with a life of unselfish service.

For himself with his devoted Queen he chose the joys of the countryside whenever his heavy State duties would permit. It was as a family man that most people best remembered him. His happy family life gave him the strength he so greatly needed for his task and was an inspiration to his people.

On that sad day the nation's sorrowing sympathy went to the gracious lady who was for 29 years his devoted partner.

The summer months - his last summer - were gladdened for the King and Queen by the birth of a grand-daughter, Princess Anne. Now her mother was our Queen Elizabeth and her brother Prince Charles heir to the throne. With the birth of the grandchildren the happy family would have been complete.

The new Queen of England returns to London from East Africa after being told of her father's death.

It was in Kenya at the Royal Hunting Lodge that the news of the King's death reached his daughter. When she returned from a night in the forest it was to learn that she was the Queen of England, acceding her father's throne immediately. As history dictates, there was to be no break in the continuity of the British monarchy. It was her decision to return to London at once.

In London, Guards of Honour from the three armed services took up their positions in Palace Yard, Westminster, in the shadow of Parliament close by the Great Hall. In the sombre grey the catafalque was the only island of colour.

The great brass cross from the Abbey, the candles from the Tomb of the Unknown Warrior, the coffin draped in his Royal Standard and the brilliant uniforms of his guards were the centrepiece in an endless stream of his mourning subjects.

At short intervals the guards changed, perfect in their precision, moving in their pageantry and oblivious to the passing throng of mourners.

Of George VI it was written..."This was a King his people loved." The King rested safe in their keeping till the long last journey to Windsor began.

From the Great Hall in the Palace of Westminster they bore George VI as the hour sounded for his last journey. In three days 300,000 of his people made their pilgrimage. Now, Britain was to bury her King and the nations came to pay their homage. On his coffin were the emblems of Majesty; the crown; the cross-mounted orb, symbol of Christianity all over the world; and the sceptre, ensign of kingly power and justice, and with them his wife's wreath of Lilies of the Valley and orchids.

Tragic in sombre black, the ladies of his house followed, the Queen, the Queen Mother and Princess Margaret together in their grief. Out of Palace Yard for the last time passed George VI whom history named 'The good'. As the coffin left Westminster on a gun carriage, Big Ben rang out, one beat a minute to mark the 56 years of the King's life.

Behind the Queen's coach walked the four Royal Dukes, Edinburgh, Gloucester, Windsor and Kent. Passing down Whitehall, representatives of foreign states remembered those who had also died for Britain at the Cenotaph, as they made their way to the waiting train at Paddington.

As the Queens and the Princess watched, the royal coffin was carried on to the train as the King left London for Royal Windsor, home of kings for 900 years.

The Queen gave pride of place to the Queen Mother and, with her sister, followed behind her father's coffin. At that moment life was still and there was silence in all the lands he held united in the Commonwealth. The sad journey to Windsor had run its course and in a statement the Queen Mother said,

"My only wish is to continue the work we sought to do together".

Queen Elizabeth II, her mother and Princes Margaret together in their grief.

HEAT WAVE

July 1952

They're swimming in the lido
    or sitting on its brink.
The kids are making whoopee
    and the oldies are getting pink.

From out of these idle loungers
    let's pick a manly torso
that's browning rather nicely
    or maybe even more so.

It's hot in Hyde Park Corner
    so guard your eyes and nose.
It's a scorcher thoughout Britain
    so crowd beneath the rose.

**Thousands flock to
Hyde Park for a chance
to lay in the sun.**

The drip of constant water
    like rain a cooling thought.
Now let us climb to roof tops where
    Windmill girls disport.

The iceman's job has vantages,
    the one on the top asleep
his mate is working like a slave
    his customers to keep.

This City gent has got it bad
    he's nearing sunstroke fever,
but what about this foolish girl
    she thinks of buying beaver.

You'll find a lot of funny folks
    one's even put his hat on
a gallant steed that Gordon Richards
    never even sat on.

Night comes and finds them lying out,
    its cooler than the bedroom.
In Hyde Park one thing's certain sure
    you will find there's lots of headroom.

Some say sleep cool on roof tops
    or on a garden seat
but when it's hot in Britain
    keeping cool is quite a feat.

Refreshed in morning early
    to work from Bucks or Hants
this is the only way sir,
    to breathe in - er - short pants!

LONDON'S LAST TRAM

July 1952

It was goodbye to the 'old clangers' as London's last tram service came to an end.

They provided a good service to the very last day and the fare taken on Tram One was donated to the Infantile Paralysis Fund.

Our picture shows the last tram just arriving from Woolwich at the New Cross Depot. London ran her first tram 91 years ago and it was indeed a worthwhile investment for London's money.

"Well now you've missed the last No. 40 for the last time."

Great Grandpa would say that there wasn't much you could do in the back seat of a car that you couldn't do on the old trams. They had a wonderful sway about them.

Travellers congregate for a place in history as they watch the London trams make their last journey.

ANTHONY EDEN WEDS

August 1952

From Downing Street, Jeanne Heal reported on the romance of the year, the wedding of Anthony Eden and the Premier's niece, Clarissa Spencer Churchill.

Mr and Mrs Churchill made their way to the wedding at Caxton Hall. The groom, who had already arrived, was wearing a navy blue suit with a grey tie and a white carnation and carrying the famous Homburg hat.

As Mr Eden faced the barrage of cameras, the gaiety of the crowd had proved that it was a truly joyous occasion for everyone. The bride arrived and the crowd caught its first glimpse of the young woman whose marriage had captured everyone's imagination. She looked radiant, wearing an orchid pink dress in silk shantung with a large spray of orchids instead of a bouquet.

The simple ceremony surrounded by flowers from Mr Churchill's garden was soon over and down the red carpet walked Mr & Mrs Eden. Cameras flashed again and a woman in the crowd pressed a silver horseshoe from her own wedding cake into the groom's hand, summing up everyone's good wishes.

Mr and Mrs Churchill at the wedding of their niece to Anthony Eden.

THE LYNMOUTH DISASTER

August 1952

One minute Lynmouth was a peaceful holiday resort; the next it was a ruin. Pathe cameraman Bill Jordan was on the spot soon after floods had swept down from the hills destroying the little town and this was his story.

"I knew very little about Lynmouth before I arrived. When I looked around I was almost glad I didn't. Friends had sent me picture postcards of Watersmeet, a beauty spot only a few miles away, it looked very pretty and quiet. It was this stream, swollen with rain, that became a raging torrent and it was these boulders that were swept down to Lynmouth to destroy shops, hotels and homes. In one single night the main street had become a wild churning river, it was dark red from the Devon soil.

When I was there nobody could tell for certain how many had been killed, we knew it was at least 22. They told me of the awful speed with which the flood struck and of the dreadful sound of the water roaring and smashing it's way through their homes.

Already work has begun to mend the battered town; the army is there and with them the men of the St. John Ambulance and the women of the W.V.S. just as they were during the Blitz. Help has been generously given. Nearby villagers have opened their homes to give shelter to the homeless.

Broken furniture littered the streets. As I stepped over the rubble to leave Lynmouth a great dark cloud hung over the little town. Slowly rain began to fall again."

Thousands are left homeless and, as well as 22 killed, 11 others are missing.

There was no time to flee when rivers burst their banks causing devasting floods to rush through Lynmouth.

THE FARNBOROUGH TRAGEDY

September 1952

MANY DIE AS DH110 CRASHES AMONG THE CROWD AFTER SMASHING SOUND BARRIER

For five days Britain and the world turned to Farnborough to marvel at the flying machines representing man's obsession to fly higher and faster. As visitors observed the latest aircraft that swept Britain to the forefront of aviation they remembered the men behind the scenes, whose initiative and inspiration had created them on their drawing boards, the men who flew them first, like John Derry, test pilot of the De Havilland 110.

The crowds that watched during those five days could never have known the thoughts of the men whose job it was to take an aircraft through the sound barrier again and again and, as they thrilled to their daring, could almost forget that on each and every flight the possibility of death flew with them, too.

Visitors who were there on the 6th day, however, would never forget, for it was on that day that a fault developed in Derry's aircraft.

While flying over the Farnborough Air Show, the De Havilland fell apart and plummeted into the crowd just after it had broken the sound barrier. The wreckage of one of the engines caused most of the casualties and 26 people were killed.

John Derry flying the De Havilland 110 over a crowd of 150,000 at the Farnborough Air Show.

Almost immediately after the tragedy, Derry's friend, Neville Duke, flew a Hawker Hunter through the sound barrier again, to prove that flying, like progress, must not stop.

John Derry was like an explorer in an unknown world whose barriers could be penetrated only by such men as he. Their courage and skill had won great victories in the skies which lived on long after their deaths.

The jet aircraft plummeted into the crowd, seconds after breaking the sound barrier. Sixty-five were injured and 26 died together with John Derry and his observer, 24 year-old Anthony Richards.

JOHN COBB DIES

October 1952

GALLANT ATTEMPT ON THE WORLD

WATER SPEED RECORD ENDS IN

TRAGEDY - FILMED BY PATHE

CAMERAMAN JOCK GEMMELL

**52-year-old John Cobb
as he prepares to break
the world water
speed record.**

John Cobb died on the waters of Loch Ness, fighting as always to win new glories for Britain. Only two days before, the Queen Mother went to meet the man called "the fastest man on earth", who tried to become the fastest man on water for Britain.

In his new jet boat the 'Crusader', Cobb had already touched a high speed during trials and there seemed no reason why yet another world speed record should not be his. Summing up everyone's thoughts, the Queen Mother wished John Cobb 'Good Luck' in his new challenge.

For six weeks the Crusader had been at Loch Ness. At dawn each day John Cobb waited for the weather to clear and his wife would always wait with him.

Then when the Loch was calm and the wind slight, Cobb would climb aboard the Crusader and a few minutes later the shrill whine of his jet engines would signal that another attempt on the world's water speed record would be made.

On those cold mornings, Cobb took the 'Crusader', out into the dark centre of the Loch.

The official timekeepers took their places
as the silver boat made its way to the start
of the measured mile, as the spectators on the
banks held their breath and echoed the words
of the Queen Mother 'Good Luck, John Cobb'.

Time and again Cobb made the run,
striving as he had done throughout his life for
new honours in the world of speed.
One day it was reported that he had
touched 185 miles an hour and everyone
was certain he would do it.

The afternoon of the day that was to be his last, Cobb took 'Crusader' along the measured mile again faster and faster until he was travelling at 240 miles an hour and then ...disaster.

The boat lifted in the air after hitting three pressure waves and then plunged into the water, smashing it apart, scattering wreckage along its wake.

There on the waters of Loch Ness John Cobb was found. The glories that he had won during his lifetime were not just for himself but for his country. For John Cobb was, above all, a great Englishman.

HARROW TRAIN CRASH

October 1952

On a misty October morning tragedy came to North London. While a local train was standing at Harrow & Wealdstone station crowded with workers on their way to the City, the Perth night express came thundering in. Then, to add to the horror, the Liverpool-bound train roared in at 60mph ploughing into the wreckage.

The injured and the dying laid there - typists, clerks, soldiers, fathers, mothers and children. It was like a battlefield, reported the cameraman who would rather have gone into battle again than film tragic scenes like those he had witnessed.

And as in all such moments of anguish mankind was at its finest. Immediately, the magnificent police and firemen, the men of the services, the women of Wealdstone, the doctors and nurses arrived on the scene. From nearby came American servicemen with specialist equipment but, even more importantly, with great hearts.

There was no panic as the people suffered. They showed great strength. They had learned to endure and in all the grief and agony there was always thought for others in deeper plight. Everyone who saw those pictures mourned for the bereaved families. Their sympathies went out to the hundreds of people whose memories had been scarred forever with the horrors of that terrible morning. But they knew that the nation was proud indeed of the courage and bravery which shone through that morning in October.

The women of Wealdstone help to aid the 200 injured and 46 critical victims of the horrific train crash.

Among twisted rails, upended coaches and shattered locomotives, rescue teams use cutting gear to search for victims under the 50-foot pile of debris. The disaster claimed 112 lives.

Ceremonious celebration at the opening of the Olympic Games at Helsinki.

Entertaining News

Amid all the stories of global tension; of natural as well as man-made disasters, Pathe News kept up a steady stream of lighter stories which amused and delighted cinema audiences of the day.

1952 had its fair share of sporting events, with Pathe covering events from the Olympic Games at Helsinki and 17-year-old 'Little Mo's' win at Wimbledon, to a day on the golfing green with Bob Hope and Bing Crosby.

The entertainment industry flourished with events from the Miss World contest held at the Lyceum, to the ceremonious joy of Christmas at St.Paul's Cathedral - all these and more have been captured by the Pathe cameramen in the following pages.

Britain wins gold as the show jumping team's Colonel Harry Llewellyn and Foxhunter jump a clear round.

HELSINKI OLYMPICS

The Olympic Games, held in Finland's magnificient new stadium, was opened with their greatest Olympian, Paavo Nurmi, lighting the flame.

In Helsinki the Olympics were dominated by Emil Zatopek, the 29-year-old Czech runner who had captured the world stage during the London Olympics in 1948. At Helsinki he retained his 10,000 metres title, won the 5,000 metres and triumphed in his first ever marathon. And to top off his record-breaking effort, his wife Dana set an Olympic record for the javelin by 15 feet.

For the British, though, the Games will be long remembered as one in which they almost failed to win a single medal. It was not until a quarter of an hour before the closing ceremony that Colonel Harry Llewellyn and Foxhunter jumped a clear round to give the show jumping team the Prix des Nations title.

Emil Zatopek leads from Alain Mimoun of France as he wins another Olympic gold medal for Czechoslovakia in the 10,000 metres.

WIMBLEDON LADIES FINAL

July 1952

Seventeen year-old Maureen 'Little Mo' Connolly, champion of America, had captured the world's admiration. Her opponent was Louise Brough, three times champion at Wimbledon. She was the only one to have beaten 'Little Mo' since she won the American title in 1951.

Maureen won the first set 7-5. A crowd of 17,000 watched as Louise Brough served from the far end. So far 50 spectators had collapsed from the heat. Nearing the end of the match, Maureen placed one wide of Louise Brough and they both waited for the verdict that would have meant victory to 'Little Mo' but the linesman ruled it out and they resumed play.

Maureen Connolly served with the world title within her grasp, forcing Miss Brough all over the court. Louise netted and Maureen Connolly became champion at her first Wimbledon appearance.

'Little Mo' was overcome. Fibrositis had threatened to put her out of the game but when the Duchess of Kent handed her the trophy, it looked as if it would be a long time before anyone took it away from her.

'Little Mo', determined to beat current Wimbledon Champ, Louise Brough.

As the Duchess of Kent looks on, a jubilant Maureen Connolly proudly displays her Wimbledon trophy to the cheering crowds.

The SS 'United States'
arrives at Southampton,
winning the Blue Riband
after her first trip across
the Atlantic.

BLUE RIBAND - FIRST TRY

July 1952

After clipping 10 hours off the 'Queen Mary's'; Atlantic crossing record, the 'United States' became the fastest liner in the world, as she proudly approached Le Havre to make her first docking in Europe.

Since the 'Queen Mary' set her record 14 years ago, big advances had been made. Builder William Gibb had a free hand in the new ship's design, with results that had made Commodore Harry Manning the happiest skipper afloat.

After leaving Le Havre bound for Southampton, the 'United States', guided by British radar, had to drive through a blinding gale to win the Blue Riband. The official run was from Ambrose Light, New York to the lonely Bishop's Rock Light off Land's End, 2,942 miles which she covered in 3 days 10 hours 40 minutes, averaging just over 35 knots. With England in sight, the 'United States' identified herself to the coastguards, otherwise they might not have known who she was. Although only 30ft shorter, she was 28,000 tons smaller than the 'Queen Mary'.

Approaching the home port of the two great Atlantic Queens where she was to receive a truly British welcome, the 'Queen Elizabeth' speeded up her turnround by 24 hours for the occasion. The traditional brooms were to go up if she beat the record both ways. Nobody knew of what the 'Queen Elizabeth' was capable, as she had never had a crack at the record before, but there was no question of a battle of the Atlantic. Reports said that, with the record won, the 'United States' would settle down to the 30 knot service of the 'Queens'.

From the great Ocean Terminal at Southampton, the Atlantic gateway to Britain, hearty congratulations were given to a sprightly youngster that had started life with a big splash.

The triumphant 'United States' is greeted by cheering crowds.

GERMAN GRAND PRIX

August 1952

It was the start of the German Grand Prix and there were plenty of good drivers in the battle.

Up in front a duel had taken place between Farina in 102 and Ascari in 101, both in Ferraris. Ascari had won the race in the last two years and once more he was the first to cross the line, giving him the Grand Prix hat trick at record speed.

Speeding round the track - with a wheel missing; some drivers had trouble keeping their car together.

An excited crowd greet Ascari - winner of the Grand Prix for the third consecutive year.

JOKE-A-STROKE GOLF

September 1952

This was a game of golf with a difference. Bob Hope, together with the 'old groaner' himself, Bing Crosby, were at Temple Golf Club, Maidenhead to play an America versus Britain match. Before they started the usual Bing/Bob backchat took place.

"Are you in form for today?"

"Oh, I'm in fine shape, I've had my second cup of tea with a dash of adrenalin and I'm ready ."

"You know I think you ought to get along home, you're starting to look like your passport picture."

"Isn't that something, I look like Bela Lugosi with Peter Lorre's head, don't I ? You should see my passport picture. You know how most passport pictures make you look like you're looking through a porthole. Mine looks like I'm sick and can't get the porthole open."

"I say, we ought to get our competitors in here, don't you think? "

"Here's Ted Ray, a fine English comic who's on his way to Korea to entertain tomorrow. Let's give him a hand."

Hope and Crosby,
delighting the crowds
with their comic rivalry.

"And here is Mr Donald Peers.

Do you think we're going to beat these boys Donald?"

"I think so."

"I think YOU are, I'm not."

"Isn't this wonderful being here in California. I just love it, look at that sky it's the only place in the world where you can get four seasons in one day. We'd better hurry, it will be snowing before the third hole, you know.

Let's move on old boy"

Before a crowd of almost 10,000 the match held at Temple Golf Club began. Donald Peers teed off and his wise-cracking partner Ted Ray seemed to approve but Bing was taking no chances. Bob said Ted Ray could do with a driving lesson. Bing had a bash; heaven and the crowd only knew where it went! Crosby took cover as the game warmed up.

The crowd made it look like a game of rugby not golf. Caught hard and fast in the middle of a dense crowd of fans, the two crooners who looked anything but rivals, made their way to the next green. Nobody seemed to worry much about the game - they only wanted to see the stars. The crowd stopped breathing and Bob teed off again. Eight of the holes had been abandoned because of the time taken to force their way through the crowd. Despite the fact that it was more like an assault course than a golf course, the four stars were still in terrific form and were really giving the crowd their money's worth.

The proceeds from the match were given to the Variety Club of Great Britain, which in turn donated to the funds of the National Playing Fields Association. By the way, if you want to know which team won the match, it was Donald Peers and Ted Ray, so they say.

Bing Crosby and Bob Hope with Ted Ray and Donald Peers before their 'assault' match.

BRMs SCOOP POOL

Three BRMs were entered for the 'Daily Graphic' Goodwood trophy and Raymond Mays, 'father' of the cars, chatted with Gonzales, one of the drivers, before the race.

Ken Wharton was another of the BRM team and Reg Parnell completed the trio as they came up to the start...and then they were off on the 36-mile course.

To the crowd's delight the BRMs were in the lead right away with Gonzales already setting a good pace out in front. Reg Parnell was well placed with Ken Wharton, number 7, close behind. Whitehead in an ERA challenged but Raymond Mays saw the BRMs making good in this, their last but one race before they were sold.

The 'Daily Graphic' Goodwood Trophy, a victorious win for Gonzales and the BRMs.

Reg Parnell in the lead from Ken Wharton.

The cars hadn't had much success in the three years they had been racing but Gonzales came in to win just behind an ERA that was still being lapped. Parnell and Wharton were second and third to Gonzales to bring victory at last to the BRMs.

**Miss Sweden wins the
Miss World title.**

MISS WORLD

November 1952

Competing for the title of 'Miss World' were eleven lovelies from all over the globe. The contest, organised by Mecca Dancing and sponsored by the 'Sunday Dispatch' was held at the Lyceum in London and was reported by Pathe on the spot.

Richard Todd and Glynis Johns were two of the judges and on that night the judging panel had a difficult task to decide on a winner.

May Louise Flodin, otherwise known as Miss Sweden, was judged after Miss Finland, but there was extra special enthusiasm when one of Britain's representatives, Marlene Dee, made her way on to the stage.

All the beauties gathered for the last time as the judges made their decision. Did you pick the winners? Well, the three lovely answers were - Miss Sweden, (18 year-old May Louise Flodin), won the title of Miss World, Miss Switzerland was second and Miss Germany third.

CHRISTMAS PIE

December 1952

In the great Cathederal of St. Pauls,
the University of London Choir gathered
to tell the story of the first Christmas.

Yes, Christmas is the time for fun
    as it has always been;
come on now, join a party
    for stars of stage and screen.

A kiss from Margaret Lockwood,
    Norman Wisdom thinks it's swell.
Joan Rice is next to hand out gifts.
    Hey 'mind my little gal'

A Happy Christmas say the stars
    to each and everyone.
But on we go to make quite sure
    we get our shopping done.

Now how about your girlfriend,
    Do you think she'd like this mink?
It's silver blue from Canada
    the price will make you blink.

Let's move on fast to Bond Street
    though I doubt it's cheaper there,
we'll try to buy some jewellery,
    thank you Commissionaire.

Well now we're in what shall we choose,
    I say it's rather swank.
Can't you feel the overdraft
    that's whistling round your bank.

That's £7,000 worth
    she's got around her neck.
The only way I could pay is
    by India Rubber cheque.

At this "picturegoer" party,
    Richard Todd's another guest.
But pick out the stars for yourself,
    I'll take a moment's rest.

£4,000 you need for those.
　　Now from the deepest vaults
come these gems worth £30,000.
　　Quick, bring the smelling salts.

Now we're getting near my mark
　　they're only half a dollar.
"Real pearls and diamonds, here you are"
　　you'll hear the salesman holler.

But I can't buy, I'm short of cash
　　... ah, there's the blooming rub.
So let's move on to somewhere else
　　...oh, there's some lovely grub.

Yes Christmas time is turkey time
　　so come on get your dough out,
we ought to buy a few of these
　　and have a darn good blow out.

But most of all it's for the kids
　　that Christmas is a joy
and what a time they have had for weeks
　　examining each toy.

And in the windows of the shops
　　they watch the grand display
to find the one, the special one,
　　they want on Christmas day.

1952

Lifestyle

Newly built 'People's houses' improve the lifestyle of British families.

Lifestyle in 1952

In Britain, 1952 brought about little change to the hardships that were familiar in everyone's lifestyle. The Budget raised taxes, cut food subsidies and raised the Bank Rate to 4 percent.

Although the struggle to strive for a better future seemed continuous, encouraging signs were becoming evident. New and innovative methods to improve 'lifestyle' at home were introduced and British Industry was experiencing gradual recovery.

The first two 'peoples' houses' were built at Desford, Leicestershire in 12 weeks for less than £1,000.

These houses seemed to be the answer to the housing drive and the Minister for Housing, Mr Harold Macmillan was now ready to inspect them with the architect, Mr Appleton.

The needs of the average housewife were considered in the design which incorporated living-room, dining-annexe and kitchen downstairs, three bedrooms upstairs and luxury built-in cupboards.

Ant chair designed by Arne Jacobsen, manufactured by Fritz Hansen, Denmark.

100,000 cotton workers idle in Lancashire

Rent and Wages in 1952
Average Rent   12/6
Average Wage   £7/11/-

Range of
Margrethe bowls by
Sigvard Bernadotte
and Acton Bjorn.

These girls are off to
the Continent, for only
£5 return, on their new
lightweight scooters
weighing only 12 stone.

National census reveals that
Britons are living longer,
marrying earlier, divorcing more
frequently and drifting away from
the traditional manufacturing
industries. One household in
three still lacks a bath, while one
in twenty has no piped water.

£30

CONTINENTAL DELICATESSEN
HIGH CLASS PROVISIONS
PROMPT DELIVERY

Food prices set to rise

Designed for those who enjoy the taste of Europe, this delicatessen in Soho is filled with specialities from the Continent.

Grocery Prices in 1952

Potatoes	2d per lb
Butter (rationed)	4s per lb
Milk	7d per pint
Meat (rationed)	2s per lb
Bacon (rationed)	4s per lb
Ground Rice	1s per lb
Tea	2s 6d per lb
Beer	1s 2d per pint

Cheese ration is cut to an ounce a week from 20th April.

The local streets were a popular place for outdoor activities.

Government announces increase in meat ration to 1/7d a week.

After a lovely summer, freak storms bring ample rain to the drought-stricken countryside but at the village of Staplecross there wasn't a drop.

Villagers queue eagerly to get a gallon of water for each coupon they have, providing precious little for a household.

Government announces end of tea rationing

68

British headmasters criticise the new GCE exams, claiming the standard is too high for some pupils.

A Science teacher explains the method of reconstructing an old car engine to his students.

The latest in hat
fashions - the
'Cleopatra' - in green
velour softened by
two-tone veil.

Pringle fashions, made
in Scotland, are in
popular demand.

Tax on clothes cut.

Clothes Prices in 1952	
Dress	65/11
Raincoat	£3/19/6
Boy's suit	37/6
Man's suit	£3/15/-
Coat	£3/19/6
Skirt	23/11

This young girl models a coat made of Britain's purest wool tartan with velvet collar and cuffs.

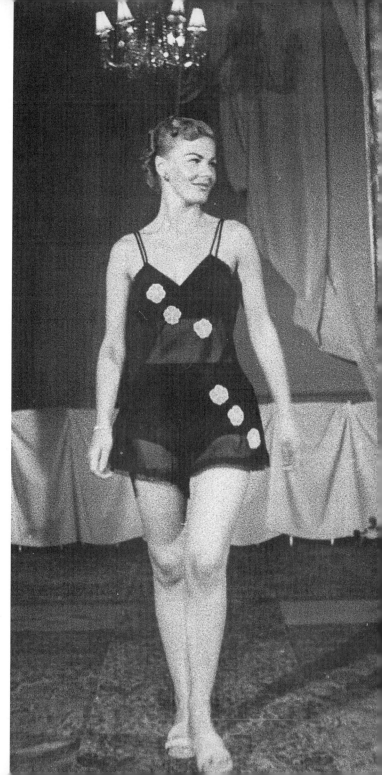

A daring number on the catwalk - black camisole and French knickers.

1952

Entertainment

Among a host of celebrities is Jack Warner, celebrating Christmas in London.

'Road to Bali'

Bing Crosby, Bob Hope,

Dorothy Lamour

Silent movie greats, Buster
Keaton and Charlie Chaplin,
team up in Chaplin's film,
'Limelight', which also
starred Claire Bloom.

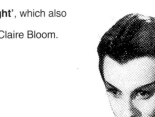

World of Entertainment

To the delight of overwhelming audiences round the country,
Hollywood made its way to Britain and Pathe News captured the
imagination of millions with its pictorials of the glamorous people
of the entertainment industry.

London's theatres were the venue for top rating plays featuring well-
known movie stars and the U.K. Box Office films were attracting
crowds to the cinema. The younger generation was showing an
increasing enthusiasm for music which developed with the release of
the first-ever Music Chart.

'Robin Hood'

Richard Todd and Joan Rice.

**Micro 16 Camera
manufactured by
W. M. Whittaker
Co. Ltd. , USA,
c/1950s.**

Charlie Chaplin visits London for the first time in 23 years with his wife Oona for the World Premier of **'Limelight'**.

'Room for One More'

Cary Grant and Betsy Drake

'Pat and Mike'

Katherine Hepburn and

Spencer Tracy

Academy Awards

21st March

Best Actress

Vivien Leigh

'Streetcar named Desire',

(also starring Marlon Brando)

Best Actor

Humphrey Bogart

'The African Queen'

Best Picture

'An American in Paris'

Best Director

George Stevens

'A Place in the Sun'

Best Supporting Actor

Karl Malden

'Streetcar named Desire'

Best Supporting Actress

Kim Hunter

'Streetcar named Desire'

Cecil B. De Mille's,

'The Greatest Show on Earth'

is the No.1 film at the U.K. Box

Office, starring Betty Hutton

and Charlton Heston, with guest

appearances by

Dorothy Lamour, Bing Crosby

and Bob Hope.

British pioneer Charles Smith

introduces the first feature movie

to use stereoscopic projection

also known as '3-dimension'

or 3-D in **'Bwana Devil'**.

Best Films in 52 - U.K. Box Office

1. The Greatest Show on Earth
2. Where no Vultures Fly.
3. Son of Paleface.
4. Ivanhoe.
5. Mandy.
6. The Planter's Wife
7. The Quiet Man
8. The World in His Arms
9. Angels One Five
10. Reluctant Heroes

'Singin' in the Rain'

starring Gene Kelly and
Debbie Reynolds is credited
as the best musical
ever made.

5th January

'Much Ado About Nothing'

John Gielgud

15th March

'The Vortex'

Noel Coward

12th April

'The Tempest'

Ralph Richardson

10th May

'Under the Sycamore Tree'

Alec Guiness and

Diana Churchill

7th June

Lena Horne at the Palladium

5th July

Jack Benny at the Palladium

September

Noel Coward's play **'Quadrille'**

opens in London

Richard Attenborough
plays the Detective,
alongside Sheila Sim.

13th September

Bob Hope at the Palladium

November 1952

Agatha Christie's play

'The Mousetrap' opens

in London at the

Ambassadors Theatre.

8th November

Max Bygraves at the Palladium

8th November

Maurice Chevalier at

the Hippodrome

21st November

'My Love & Devotion'

Doris Day

14th November

First-ever British Music

Chart printed in

'New Musical Express'.

Here we show a selection

of the Top 12 that appeared

on that day.

You Belong To Me	Jo Stafford	14th November	19	wks	No. 1
Here In My Heart	Al Martino	14th November	18	wks	No. 1
Feet Up	Guy Mitchell	14th November	10	wks	No. 2
Because You're Mine	Mario Lanza	14th November	24	wks	No. 3
Isle Of Innisfree	Bing Crosby	14th November	12	wks	No. 3
Half As Much	Rosemary Clooney	14th November	9	wks	No. 3
Somewhere Along The Way	Nat King Cole	14th November	7	wks	No. 3
High Noon	Frankie Laine	14th November	7	wks	No. 7
Forget Me Not	Vera Lynn	14th November	1	wk	No. 7
Sugarbush	Doris Day &				
	Frankie Laine	14th November	2	wks	No. 8
Blue Tango	Ray Martin	14th November	1	wk	No. 8
Homing Waltz	Vera Lynn	14th November	3	wks	No. 9
Auf Wiedersehen	Vera Lynn	14th November	1	wk	No.10
Cowpunchers Cantata	Max Bygraves	14th November	1	wk	No.11
Walking My Baby Back Home	Johnnie Ray	14th November	1	wk	No.12

(The Top twelve included more than one entry at some chart positions).

5th December

'Zing a little Zong'

Bing Crosby &

Jane Wyman

19th December

'Walkin' to Missouri'

Tony Brent

19th December

'White Christmas'

Mantovani

19th November

'Because You're Mine'

Nat King Cole

21st November

'Take my Heart'

Al Martino

**Al Martino shot
to No.1 with
'Here in My Heart'.**

19th December

'Jambalaya'

Jo Stafford

19th December

'Silent Night'

Bing Crosby

5th December

'Come A-long A-love'

Kay Starr

Zenith Transoceanic
Radio, Zenith Radio
Corporation, USA,
early 1950s.

Teenagers dance to
their favourite hits at
a popular dance club.

12th December

'Brittania Rag'

Winifred Atwell

19th December

'Takes Two to Tango'

Louis Armstrong

Gilbert Harding clashes with
Eamonn Andrews, Chairman
of 'What's my Line'.

29th September

Dynamic Hollywood star Betty
Hutton visits the Poplar Boys'
Club in Bermondsey, a gift of
the Variety Club of Great Britain.

The club, which provides
recreation for boys who would
otherwise play in the streets,
gives her a warm welcome.

**Hollywood stars and producers
flood into England.**

Jack L. Warner who, with his
brothers, made the cinema the
greatest medium of entertainment.

Despite belief that sound could
not succeed, the Warner Brothers
made the first talkies with
Al Jolson.

Tallulah Bankhead tells all
in her sensational memoirs.

Rita Hayworth drops divorce
proceedings against Aga Khan.

Clark Gable admits to being too
old for love!

The SS "United
States" brings its
liveliest passenger
into Southampton -
yes, it's Bob Hope.

Cinerama launched at the
Broadway Theatre, New York.

The stars come out in the daytime for the 'Sunday Pictorial' Film Garden Party held at Morden Hall Park, Surrey. And to meet their favourites (Joan Rice and Veronica Hurst among them) are 25,000 fans.

Children's charities benefit from the proceeds of the party, so to help comes Jimmy Edwards. Still talking shop are Richard Todd and Maureen O'Neill.

Richard Attenborough tries his strength in the fairground. He'll need all he's got among the crowds. It's the battle of the fans - with the stars as prizes !

Hollywood film star Errol Flynn arrives in Britain to make a film.

1952

War & Politics

Korean Prisoner of War Camp.

**Andrei Gromyko is
appointed Soviet
Ambassador to Britain.**

**Iain Macleod is
appointed Minister
of Health.**

War & Politics

Although the official end to World War II in the Pacific was announced,
Britain experienced the escalation of political unrest in the Middle East
while in Kenya, troops were sent to control the uprising of the
Mau Mau terrorists.

In Korea the allies waged heavy bombing raids to destroy the
enemy's ability to mount a large-scale offensive. Later, on Cheju Island
off south-west Korea, trouble mounted at the Prisoner of War Camp,
as Communist members launched an active demonstration resulting
in US guards opening fire to control the riot.

In 1952 there was no end to the war in Korea and the United
Nations and Britain strengthened their relationship as growing
concerns over Western foreign policies and world problems were
frequently discussed.

**20,000 NHS doctors get
a pay rise of £500 a year
backdated to 1948.**

**Prisoners of War
are detained
after violent
demonstrations.**

**Equal pay for women
doing the same jobs
as men is given
full support in the
House of Commons.**

The Navy's first operational helicopter squadron 848 will soon be leaving the Royal Naval Station, Gosport to assist in jungle attacks against the bandits in Malaya.

The Sikorsky helicopters, sent from America, will soon be shipped to Malaya (along with 14 officers and 80 ratings) to carry British troops into battle and to

Helicopter squadron 848 shipped to Malaya.

evacuate the wounded from the jungle.

Accredited with a brilliant record as a tough fighter and skilled general, the newly - appointed High Commissioner for Malaya, General Sir Gerald Templar, (right), is given the job of putting an end to the fighting there.

Off coast of Korea, 26
die as U.S. troops
battle with prisoners.

Itzhak Ben-Zvi
becomes the
President of Israel.

French casualties from
attack on Viet Minh
in Vietnam.

Through the jungles of Indo-China, French paratroopers fall back from the Black River as hoards of Communist rebel forces strike hard along the 100-mile front. This is perhaps the fiercest onslaught yet directed by the Viet Minh and French troops welcome a brief respite from the savage battle.

Overhead, an aircraft dives on the enemy; the attack is on again. Quickly the weary paratroopers hurry to their position to engage the rebels once more.

The fighting goes on, while the wounded are given attention. Casualties are heavy in face of a fanatical enemy of superior numbers, who are familiar with the country.

To transfer the wounded to hospitals behind the lines, a small clearing is made in the jungle, and now a helicopter flies in, despite enemy fire, on its mission of mercy.

Hurriedly the helicopter leaves the battlefront but soon it will return to pick up more of the wounded. In the meantime, the French move forward to strike again at the Viet Minh terrorists.

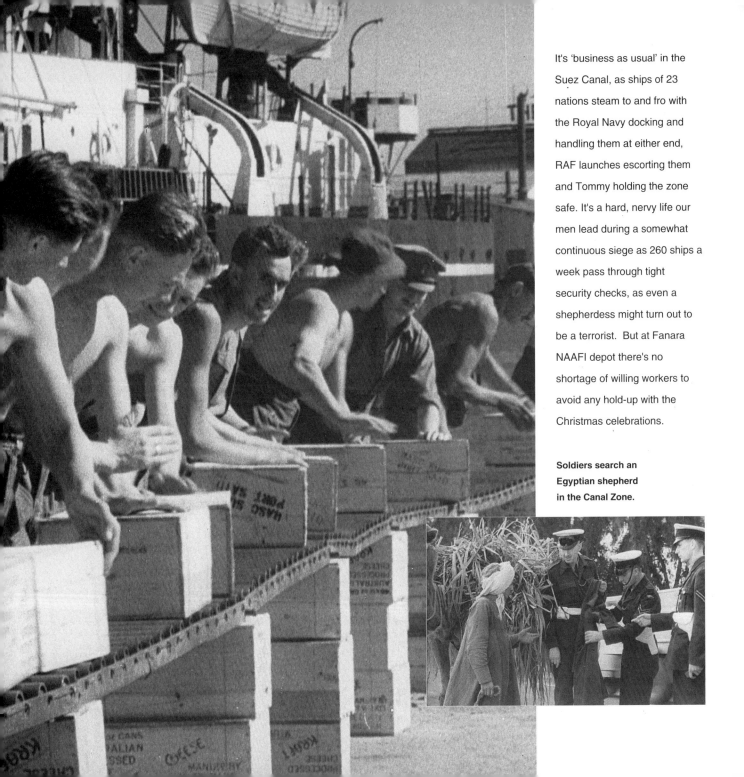

It's 'business as usual' in the Suez Canal, as ships of 23 nations steam to and fro with the Royal Navy docking and handling them at either end, RAF launches escorting them and Tommy holding the zone safe. It's a hard, nervy life our men lead during a somewhat continuous siege as 260 ships a week pass through tight security checks, as even a shepherdess might turn out to be a terrorist. But at Fanara NAAFI depot there's no shortage of willing workers to avoid any hold-up with the Christmas celebrations.

Soldiers search an Egyptian shepherd in the Canal Zone.

U.S. guards kill 52
rioting Chinese POWs.

Riots in Cairo -
100 dead.

Haile Selassie signs
declaration that
federates his country
with Eritrea.

Field Marshall Sir
William Slim is
appointed Govenor-
General of Australia.

West Germany agrees
to pay Israel £293
million in restitution
for Nazi atrocities.

President Truman
marks the official end
of World War II in
the Pacific.

Delegates arrive at the Winter Gardens in Morecambe, Lancashire, to attend the Labour Party's annual conference and Trade Union chiefs Arthur Deakin and Sir William Lawther, the miners' leader, have come to the aid of their party.

The boss himself, Mr Attlee saw his party rival, Aneurin Bevan, triumph over him as his fiery speech upsets his fellow Socialists who see a threat to the security of Mr Attlee and his followers. A vote to select the National Executive is taken and results in the election of Mr Bevan and many of his supporters.

The Bevanites strengthen their position on the Labour's National Executive with the election of Harold Wilson.

1952

Births, Deaths & Marriages

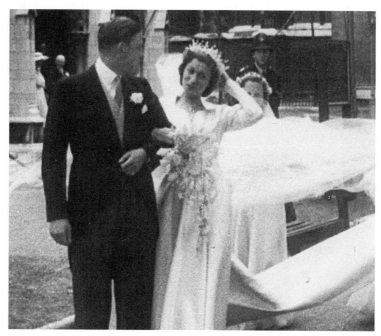

The Queen's cousin, the Hon. Gerald Lascelles marries Miss Angela Dowding.

14th May

David Byrne

12th February

Simon McCorkindale

Births, Deaths & Marriages

Britain was plunged into sorrow and mourning when in February news from Sandringham announced that the King was dead. The heart of the nation stopped as it witnessed the passing of a monarch whose life was an inspiration to all he ruled.

As the year went on, pomp and ceremony surrounded many famous weddings and gave cause for thousands to celebrate a joyous occasion. The wedding of the year attracted 6,000 Britons to St Margaret's, Westminster as they watched the Honourable Gerald Lascelles, the Queen's cousin, marry Angela Dowding.

From Westerham Church in Kent, Jeremy Bernard Soames is carried out in his mother's arms, under his grandfather's watchful eye, after his christening. Although Master Soames doesn't know it yet, it is from his godfather, Field Marshal Viscount Montgomery, that he gets his second name, Bernard.

The christening party is held at nearby Chartwell Farm, country home of Mr Churchill, the proud grandfather.

3rd May

Alan Wells

5th February

Russell Grant

19th April

David Icke

2nd May

Isla St. Claire

21st May

Mr T - '**A-Team**'

18th June

Isabella Rossellini

Carol Kane

22nd June

Alistair Stewart

1st July

Dan Aykroyd

Dan Aykroyd in his movie role - 'Driving Miss Daisy', 1989.

22nd June

Alistair Stewart

7th June

Liam Neeson

21st July

Robin Williams

18th August

Patrick Swayze

7th August

Alexei Sayle

Patrick Swayze, star of 1989s musical love story 'Dirty Dancing', with Jennifer Grey.

22nd October

Jeff Goldblum

25 September

Christopher Reeve

25 September

Mark Hamill

Mark Hamill in New York signing autographs at an orphanage. In 1977 he starred in Hollywood's history-making 'Star Wars'.

20th October

Melanie Mayron

20th December

Jenny Agutter

Jenny Agutter (far right) in 'The Railway Children' - No. 6 at the U.K. Box Office in 1971.

3rd December

Mel Smith

We expected, as always, a year of changing fortunes. But we little thought that, so early in the year, the nation would be mourning the passing of our great King.

'Streets of Sorrow' as the procession leaves Kings Cross for Westminster Hall.

The coffin of King George VI will be watched by thousands of his mourning people as it is borne on a gun carriage from Kings Cross to Westminster Hall, after its journey by train from Sandringham.

Arriving at Kings Cross at 2.45 pm, the procession will take approximately one hour to reach Westminster Hall. The gun carriage, drawn by the King's Troop, Royal Horse Artillery, will be accompanied by the Grenadier Guards.

The Duke of Edinburgh and the Duke of Gloucester, with their suites, will walk immediately behind the gun-carriage, followed by members of his late Majesty's household.

On arrival at Westminster Hall, the coffin will be received by the Archbishop of Canterbury, the Lord Great Chamberlain, the Earl Marshal and the Minister of Works, and be carried to the catafalque.

A private service will follow and the public are admitted to pay homage over the three days before The King is laid to rest at Windsor.

A mourning subject pays tribute to the King.

Sir Stafford Cripps, the
Chancellor of the
Exchequer, who died
21st April 1952..

11th October

Jack Conway

13th February

Alfred Einstein

21st May

John Garfield

26th July

Eva Peron

8th August

The Drummond Family

20th August

Kurt Schumacher

6th September

Gertrude Lawrence

20th October

Basil Radford

10th October

Lady Derby

23rd October

Susan Peters

27th October

Gladys George

29th September

John Cobb

9th November

First President of Israel -

Dr Chaim Weizmann

8th December

Hattie McDaniel

Marriages

4th March

Ronald Reagan marries

Nancy Davis

18th March

Betty Hutton marries

Charles O'Curran

18th June

Judy Garland marries

Sidney Luft

29th April

Shelley Winters marries

Vittorio Gassman

1st August

Jack Carson marries

Lola Albright

August

Anthony Eden marries

Clarissa Spencer Churchill

It's the wedding of the year and 6,000 gather at St Margaret's, Westminster, in the hope of seeing the Queen, who unfortunately, at the last moment, is prevented from attending by a chill. Bridesmaids include Miss Mary Evans of Los Angeles, a friend of the bride.

Miss Angela Dowding is to marry the Queen's cousin, the Honourable Gerald Lascelles, who is the second son of the Princess Royal and younger brother of the Earl of Harewood. Miss Dowding, who is the step-daughter of Sir John Fox, was at one time an actress with ENSA.

With the Service now over, the bridegroom escorts his bride out to the courtyard. She wears a parchment silk satin dress designed by her mother, Lady Fox.

Now the happy couple leave for a reception at St James Palace. Though the Queen was unable to attend, other Royal guests besides the Princess Royal (mother of the groom) included Princess Margaret, the Duchesses of Gloucester and Kent and the Duke of Edinburgh.

The Honourable Gerald Lascelles and Miss Angela Dowding.

Marriages

14th August

Anthony Eden marries
Clarissa Spencer Churchill

At Caxton Hall, London, it's a different affair altogether as 19-year-old Elizabeth Taylor arrives for her wedding to Michael Wilding. Overboard went all the plans for a quiet wedding; somehow the news leaked out.

And here they are, 39-year-old Michael Wilding and his bride.

Now there's no holding the huge crowd. Michael's rung the bell of ten with his British pictures and he's one of our most popular screen stars. His romance with Elizabeth Taylor had all fans really excited. Now the Wildings are off to the Continent for their honeymoon, if they can force their way through this crowd of well-wishers.

19th November

Micky Rooney weds for a fourth time

The Earl of Airlie marries

Jean Paul Belmondo marries

Enoch Powell marries

1st November

Jane Wyman marries
Freddie Karger

24th November

Pier Angeli marries
Vic Damone

20th December

Brigitte Bardot marries
Roger Vadim.

Elizabeth Taylor marries her first husband.

February

Screen star Gracie Fields
marries Boris Alperovici at a
quiet and simple ceremony.

1952

Disasters

Horrific scenes at Harrow, amid a pile of smashed trains and smoking wreckage.

**Arsenic in talcum powder
kills 16 babies.**

**Bus hits queue
of children,
killing four.**

Disasters

Before the year's end, Britons had endured a series of disasters which claimed hundreds of lives and left painful memories of destruction and suffering.

The cameras of Pathe News were there to witness the scenes of anguish and grim devastation; the country's second worst train crash and London's worst fire since the Blitz were just some in a trail of misfortunes.

A railway disaster at Harrow and Wealdstone Station, the second worst in British train history so far, left 112 dead when a high-speed locomotive from Euston crashed into two trains that had collided in front of it moments earlier.

Commuters waiting on the platform were injured as tons of twisted track and shattered carriages hurtled into the air. Wreckage lay strewn across six tracks and a cloud of smoke shrouded all that remained of the station. Rescue teams worked from morning till night using cutting gear to get to the bottom of the 50-foot pile of smoking debris in search of victims.

**A tornado sweeps six
mid-west states in
the U.S., killing 200 and
injuring 2,500.**

**Derry's De Havilland 110
fighter fell apart over
the Farnborough Air
Show and plummeted
into the crowd, killing
26 people.**

Without warning, freak storms
hit north Devon causing
disastrous flooding to about 250
square miles. Thirty-six people
are feared dead and thousands
have been made homeless in
the resort of Lynmouth, which
was devastated when rivers
burst their banks and swept
down surrounding hills. Victims
had no time to flee as their
houses were buried beneath
the unremitting flow of mud,
rocks and debris.

A policeman carries out
vital rescue procedures
at Lynmouth.

44 die as KLM aircraft
crashes while landing
in rain and fog
at Frankfurt.

Air crash in
Thanet, Kent.

Wake Island, in the mid-
Pacific Ocean, was the
victim of one of the
worst typhoons ever
recorded, destroying
everything in its path.

84 die in world's worst
air tragedy in
Washington State.

Miraculously only
two were injured and
most of the 750
islanders were
evacuated after gales
of 160 miles an hour
left their island in total
ruin. Damage of up
to ten million dollars
was caused.

California experienced its
second earthquake within a
month, causing destruction to
the small town of Bakersfield,
85 miles from Los Angeles. For
ten seconds the ground heaved
and buildings collapsed, killing
two and injuring thirty.

The citizens of Bakersfield
faced the disaster without panic
and returned to start rebuilding
their shops and homes.

44 die as KLM aircraft
crashes while landing
in rain and fog
at Frankfurt, Germany.

Minesweeper/Destroyer
sinks in Atlantic -
176 missing.

A Dodge destroyed
by rubble after
the earthquake.

At Broad Street railway warehouse, London's firemen were fighting the City's worst fire since the Blitz. For six hours, crews fought the blaze desperately with twenty-two pumps in action. One fire engine was destroyed during the brave attempt and before the night was out, two were killed and twenty-one more were injured.

**The remains of a
fire engine after
the warehouse blaze.**

1952

Innovation

Improved bus destination blinds are put into use.

Since the first printing
press 500 years ago,
Britain introduces
the first 'speedy'
electronic transcriber.

Innovation

Since the stalemate during the war, technology forged ahead strongly
in 1952 with the adventurous and innovative men who possessed the
ideas and daring to show the world.

In Britain aviators searched for ways to build bigger and faster
aircraft and attempts were made to break the world water speed
record with the new Jet-engined speed boat.

The political world also joined the race to explore the possibilities
of advanced technology resulting in the development of the first
atomic weapons.

**At Stockholm Nobel Prizes
are awarded to the following:**

Felix Bloch and Edward Purcell
(US, Physics)

Archer Martin and
Richard Synge (UK, Chemistry)

Selman Waksman
(US, Medicine)

Francois Mauriac
(France, Literature)

And in Oslo to:

Albert Schweitzer
(France, Peace)

**Britain explodes atomic
bomb for the first time.**

**U.S.A. explodes the
H-bomb.**

**A mechanical heart was
applied successfully to
a patient for the first
time at Pennsylvania
Hospital in Philadelphia.
The device supported
Peter During, a 41-year-
old steelworker, for 80
minutes but he later
died of causes
unrelated to the use of
the equipment.**

**Fim starlet Valerie
Carlton with the
new Dishmaster -
"Does your chores at
the touch of a switch".**

Gay Coronation
pennant to fly
on your car
next year.
Price: 17s 6d.

Britain's motor
manufacturers had little
trouble competing with
cars from all over the
Continent at the Paris
Motor Show. The
prestige Aston Martin
and Jaguar Coupe were
among more than twenty
British models exhibited
to entice the European
market. The sporty
Midget MG proved a
popular model with the
more modest buyer.

Any traffic cop will tell you that the first thing every car needs is good brakes! 'Exhibit A', with these men from the Hendon Police College, is the newest brainwave in brakes - the disc brake. It's a large metal disc, vertical, and running with the wheel. Needs no adjustment, resists heat and water. After being tried out successfully in the BRM these brakes will begin to be fitted to ordinary cars. Let's see if it works.

**The Austin 'Champ',
a British-made Military
Jeep that defeats tough
land and water.**

Curious inspection -
the new 'A.C. Petite'.

Three wheels, two seats, $3\frac{1}{2}$-horse power, $1\frac{1}{2}$ d. a mile. That's the story in a nutshell of Britain's newest baby car - the 'A.C. Petite'.

At this private 'little motor show' for Pathe News, the new 'Petite' showed its form. Until now, this model has been doing its road tests disguised as a motorised invalid carriage, and by next Spring they'll be on the roads. So look right, left -

Metal fatigue discovered.

Government in talks about new independent TV station.

The Rover Jet 1, the world's first turbo-jet car, is ready for the high speed test on the Jabbeke road near Ostend. During the test she exceeded 151 miles an hour - an all-British triumph in the motoring world.

Innovation

The first four-engined delta-wing jet bomber, the Avro 'Vulcan' makes its maiden flight.

US helicopter makes first Transatlantic flight.

Britain's mammoth flying-boat, 'The Princess' becomes airborne, touching 225 miles an hour, during her first taxiing trials.

According to her pilot she handles like a jet-fighter, despite the fact that she's bigger than the mighty Brabazon.

Britain set to
dominate world
jet aircraft industry.

Prototype Vickers
Valiant - long range jet
for carrying the atomic
bomb - crashes.

A British Canberra
bomber breaks all
records with the first
Transatlantic round trip
in a single day. The
journey took 7 hours
and 59 minutes flying
from Northern Ireland to
Gander, Newfoundland
and back.

The British Overseas Airways
Corporation began the jet era
for passenger flight with its first
scheduled Comet airliner leaving
London Airport for Johannesburg
with 36 passengers on board.

The 6,724 mile journey was
expected to take 18 hours and
40 minutes.

The world's first Atomic Gun is idle now as two driving cabs take it to the firing range at Aberdeen, Maryland, U.S.A.

The unloading gun crew have their hands full with a weapon that weighs 85 tons and can hurl 12 inch shells up to 20 miles away.

The barrel's 40 feet long and after the shell is put in the proper place and rammed home, the charge is placed on the loading tray and gets the same treatment.

1952

Crime

Marie Besnard, entering the court for the last time - accused of twelve murders.

**First Juvenile Detention
Centre opens in
Oxfordshire.**

**Re-opening of the
Old Bailey in London.**

Crime

The opening of the first Juvenile Detention Centre was the first
indication that the number of criminal offences in Britain was
on the increase.

    Before the year's end, Britons witnessed the last man to be
sentenced to death by hanging. That man was Derek William Bentley,
who was convicted of murdering a police constable after a bungled
robbery. Although it was his accomplice who fired the round of shots,
Craig was reprieved of the fate met by Bentley because of his youth.

    In France, the courts were astonished with the case of a 51-year-
old woman guilty of murdering 12 persons; the alleged thirteenth
murder was dropped because it happened more than 12 years ago.

**Alicia Roberts acquitted
of murdering husband.**

**A servant runs wild
at the Earl of Derby's
home shooting dead
two butlers and
wounding the Countess.**

**West Germany -
Field Marshall Kesselring,
who has cancer, is
released from his 21-year
war crime jail term.**

**Madman escapes from
Broadmoor.**

Marie Besnard, a village woman of over 50 years of age, is accused of having murdered, by arseniate poison, twelve people of her connections and family to inherit their wealth. After 31 months of judicial enquiries to find the proof of her guilt,.she now stands before her judges. She has always denied having committed any murders but a weighty file of reports, 75 centimetres high, is before the State presenter and Judge who intend to sentence her for her deeds.

A thirteenth charge of murdering her husband Auguste Antigny has been dropped, because it is more than twelve years old but arseniate poison was also found in his remains.

Arrival of Marie Besnard, surrounded by gendarmes of her guard at the Palace of Justice.

In Bonn, outside the West German Parliament Building, an angry mob demonstrates against the German vote to join in the defence of Europe. Police use fire hoses to subdue the rioters.

Meanwhile, the 'Big Three' reach agreement with Chancellor Adenauer on Germany's role in defence and a new German Army under NATO may soon be a reality.

These scenes of violence, some German authorities say, are Communist-inspired. The police wade in with truncheons swinging and, in the end, order is restored - and Germany will re-arm.

Police arrest demonstrator at anti re-armament riot in Bonn.

Communist retaliation looms at the arrival of the Supreme Head of Western Defence.

As General and Mrs Mathew Ridgway arrive at London's Airport they are greeted by Sir John Slessor, Chief of Air Staff.

Behind them, Communist agitators start to demonstrate about the germ warfare charge which both Britain and America have labelled a lie but are foiled by security police. Before leaving America, General Ridgway (who is Supreme Head of Western Defence) was also made head of all American forces in Europe. His job is to build up the collective defence which Britain and other Western powers have chosen as the best means of safety.

**Move to ban small
fire arms.**

**Marshall accused of
giving secrets to
the Russians.**

"Let him have it Chris"

On the 11th December 1952, nineteen-year-old Derek William Bentley and Christopher Craig, aged sixteen, were found guilty of murdering Police Constable Sidney Miles on the roof of a Croydon warehouse after a bungled robbery. As a result, Bentley was sentenced to hang for the murder but his accomplice, who had fired the shots with a revolver, escaped the death penalty because of his youth.

The most serious piece of evidence against Bentley was that given by a police witness who told the court that Bentley was heard to shout "Let him have it Chris", before Craig opened fire with nine shots, although the defence claimed that the defendant had meant the gun itself.

Craig was sentenced to be detained at Her Majesty's pleasure and was described by Lord Goddard, the Lord Chief Justice, as "one of the most dangerous criminals ever to stand in the dock". Craig was also said to be a member of a gang which obtained weapons from people who kept them as war souvenirs. As a result of this serious crime, the Home Secretary planned to strengthen the laws on carrying firearms.

1952

Sport

In Helsinki, thousands watch the official opening of the XVth Olympic Games.

**The worst ever
mountaineering and
sporting disaster in
terms of fatalities,
occured in 1952 during
a Russian attempt on
Mount Everest.
Approximately 40 of the
expedition perished.**

**The Derby - Aga Khan's
horse 'Tulyar' wins with
Lester Piggott riding;
'Gay time' second.**

Sport

The year's sporting events provided inspiration and captive
entertainment as current and new sporting stars emerged, breaking
world records with amazing skill and determination.

'Little Mo' won the hearts of thousands as she triumphed to win the
Wimbledon Women's Final at seventeen. At the Helsinki Olympic
Games and Winter Olympics in Oslo, gold was brought home to
Britain by Colonel Harry Llewellyn and Foxhunter and Figure Skating
Champion Jeanette Altwegg.

British Football was becoming an increasingly popular spectator
sport and at the F.A. Cup Final, crowds gathered to watch Newcastle
United win for the second time in two years.

**Grand National won
by 'Teal'.**

Belgian Grand Prix	Ascari
French Grand Prix	Ascari
German Grand Prix	Ascari
British Grand Prix	Ascari
Dutch Grand Prix	Ascari
Canadian Grand Prix	Ascari
Swiss Grand Prix	Taruffi

**British Grand Prix
at Silverstone, won by
Ascari in Ferrari.**

Demand to put the FA
Cup Final on TV.

BOVRIL

helps you put
your best foot forward

COLLECT YOUR CUP
OF BOVRIL AT THE BAR

THE FOOTBALL ASSOCIATION CHALLENGE CUP COMPETITION
FINAL TIE
ARSENAL v NEWCASTLE UNITED
SATURDAY, MAY 3rd, 1952 KICK OFF 3pm

Here they come! Newcastle and Arsenal to battle for the Cup. It's the big North-South Final everyone would have picked for a real tussle and that's how it turned out. It's a 100,000 full house with a lot of Geordies to cheer skipper Joe Harvey and the Magpies to keep the Cup they won last year. They look to Jackie Milburn to do the trick again. Mr Churchill represents the Queen, who is in mourning.

For Newcastle George Robledo has scored five cup-tie goals.

Now he scores again for the second year in succession.

Arsenal are first to congratulate their conquerors on a great triumph. Skipper Joe Harvey receives the Cup from Mr Churchill.

Mr Arthur Ellis - Today's referee. At 36, he is one of the youngest to be honoured with an F.A. Cup Final.

THE ARSENAL PLAYERS

WALLEY BARNES
Right Back

GEORGE SWINDIN
Goalkeeper

LIONEL SMITH
Left Back

ALEC FORBES
Right Half

RAY DANIEL
Centre Half

JOE MERCER (Capt.)
Left Half

JIMMY LOGIE
Inside Right

PETER GORING
Centre Forward

DUGGIE LISHMAN
Inside Left

FREDDIE COX
Outside Right

Reserves :
REG LEWIS
CLIFF HOLTON

DON ROPER
Outside Left

THE NEWCASTLE UNITED PLAYERS

BOB COWELL
Right Back

RONNIE SIMPSON
Goalkeeper

ALFRED McMICHAEL
Left Back

JOE HARVEY (Capt.)
Right Half

FRANK BRENNAN
Centre Half

TED ROBLEDO
Left Half

BILLY FOULKES
Inside Right

JACK MILBURN
Centre Forward

GEORGE ROBLEDO
Inside Left

TOMMY WALKER
Outside Right

Reserve :
GEORGE HANNAH

BOBBY MITCHELL
Outside Left

Newcastle United become the first team since 1891 to win the FA Cup for 2 years running, beating Arsenal 1-0.

Well done Newcastle - you've done it again!

139

**Manchester United win
the League.**

It's Shrovetide in Atherstone
and time for soccer star and
local boy Nobby Wilson to start
the annual football-through-the-
streets. From three till five the
'all-in' will continue and the law
can't do anything about it.

King John started the
tradition when he threw a bag of
gold to get rid of an Atherstone
crowd. Now they use a football
and whoever holds it at five
o'clock is entitled to free drinks
in all the locals.

There must be easier ways
of earning the price of a pint!

The winner is usually
underneath the lot and he may
not survive to collect!

**England versus the
Springboks.**

Tour de France won
by F. Coppi (Italy).

Leeds won the National
Angling Championships
a record seven times
between 1909 and 1952.

Tommy Lawton signs
for Brentford.

Snow clearing at
White Hart Lane for
Arsenal v Chelsea
match.

Surrey win County Cricket Championship, for the first time since 1914.

At Lord's Cricket Ground, playing against Northamptonshire, the same county against which he scored his first century sixteen years ago, Denis Compfon hits his hundredth hundred.

Through the gates erected to the memory of W. G. Grace, this other 'Great Cricketer' comes out to meet some of those who cheered him to his triumph. It was appropriate that, playing for his county team, Denis Compton made the scoring stroke at Lord's, the scene of many of his greatest triumphs, to put him on the short list of the all-time great in cricket.

Denis Compton, the familiar face in Brylcream advertisements, hits his 100th century.

Len Hutton becomes the first ever 'paid' captain of England's cricket team.

Yorkshire fast bowler Freddie Trueman wins the Cricket Writers' Trophy as 'Best Young Cricketer of 1952'.

21 year-old Jeanette Altwegg wins Britain's first Olympic gold for Figure Skating at Oslo.

February

At Oslo the Winter Games of the VIth Olympics open in the huge Bislet Stadium as the Olympic torch arrives from Morgedal, cradle of modern skiing, to light the Olympic fllame which will burn while the Games are on. The torch is handed to a great-nephew of Dr Nansen (the famous Norwegian polar explorer) who lights the flame. Thirty nations are engaged in the Winter Games and Oslo has spared no trouble to make the Games a success.

DE VI OLYMPISKE VINTERLEKER OSLO 1952

OLYMPIC TEAMS
1952

BRITISH

OLYMPIC TEAMS
1952

**Foxhunter wins
Britain's only
Gold medal.**

Finland's capital welcomes
6,000 athletes of seventy nations
to the XVth Olympic Games.
The founder of the Games,
Greece, leads the procession
at the great Helsinki stadium
where 80,000 wait for President
Paasikivi of Finland to open
the Games.

On to the track comes
Paavo Nurmi (Finland's greatest
Olympian) bearing the torch
which was lit at Olympia in
Greece. The crowds applaud as
the flame which will burn
throughout out the Games
marks the official opening of the
XVth Olympiad.

MENS' ATHLETICS

Event	Athlete	Country	Result
100m	Lindy Remigino	USA	10.4
200m	Andrew Stanfield	USA	20.7
400m	Georges Rhoden	JAM	45.9
800m	Malvin Whitfield	USA	1:49.2
1500m	Josef Barthel	LUX	3:45.1
5000m	Emil Zatopek	TCH	14:06.6
10,000m	Emil Zatopek	TCH	29:17.0
Marathon	Emil Zatopek	TCH	2:23:03.2
110m Hurdles	Harrison Dillard	USA	13.7
400m Hurdles	Charles Moore	USA	50.8
4 x 100m Relay		USA	40.01
4 x 400m Relay		JAM	3:03.9
50km Walk	Giuseppe Dordoni	ITA	4:28.07.8
10km Walk	John Mikaelsson	SWE	45:02.08
High Jump	Walter Davis	USA	2.04
Long Jump	Gerome Biffle	USA	7.57
Triple Jump	Adhemar Ferraria Da Silva	BRA	16.22
Pole Vault	Robert Richards	USA	4.55
Shotput	Parry O'Brien	USA	17.41
Discuss	Sim Iness	USA	55.03
Hammer	Josef Csernak	HUN	60.34
Javelin	Cyrus Young	USA	73.78
Decathlon	Robert Mathias	USA	7887.

WOMENS' ATHLETICS

Event	Athlete	Country	Result
100m	Marjorie Jackson	AUS	11.5
200m	Marjorie Jackson	AUS	23.7
80m Hurdles	S. de la Hunty Strickland	AUS	10.9
4 x 100m Relay		USA	45.9
High Jump	Esther Brand	SAF	1.67
Long Jump	Yvette Williams	NZL	6.24
Shotput	Galina Zybina	URS	15.28
Discuss	Nina Romaschkova	URS	51.42
Javelin	Dana Zatopkova	TCH	50.47

**Teddy Gardner wins
European flyweight title.**

At St. James's Hall, Newcastle,
Teddy Gardner tackles Louis
Sckena for the flyweight
championship of Europe.
Gardner, the 30-year-old bald-
headed publican from West
Hartlepool, rose in the boxing
world the tough way.

After five rounds Gardner is
safely ahead on points and the
Frenchman has yet to win a
round. Gardner is one of the
smartest little boxers we've
had in years.

The fight goes to Teddy
Gardner of Hartlepool.

So if you go to Teddy's pub,
don't argue when he says
"Time, Gentlemen, please".

**Johnny Williams beats
Jack Gardner for the
heavyweight title.**

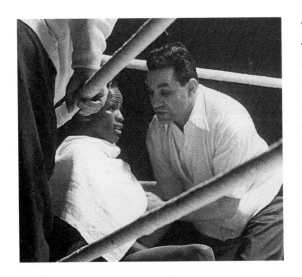

At Nottingham Ice Stadium,
Jake Tuli, 'The Zulu Kid', meets
Belgian flyweight Emile
Delplanque. The whole of Tuli's
purse tonight will go to the
widow of Honore Pratesi, who
died as a result of their fight last
month. Promoter Reg King
watches the Belgian champ
receive attention after a first
round which looked to be in
Tuli's favour.

Sugar Ray Robinson is
beaten by Maxim.

At the Royal Albert Hall, after
the parade of the mighty muscle
men, the mightiest of them all,
'Giant Gargantua' takes to the
ring. This colossal German
wrestler stands eight feet tall
and weighs fifty stone.

Randolph Turpin stops
Don Cockell in 11th
round to win the British
light/heavyweight title.

Bruce Woodcock told
not to fight again.

NORMAN MORRELL (London) Ltd. presents —
NEXT FRIDAY, AUGUST 29 at 7.30
WRESTLING
Top of the Bill
SHIRLEY CRABTREE v. ALF CADMAN
OTHER BOUTS:
NORMAN WALSH v. AL HAYES ● LES KELLETT v. JACK PROCTER
CHIC BOOTH v. ARTHUR DANIELS
Prices: 2/6 3/6 4/6 6/- 10/-
Advance Booking: Fryer Travel Bureau, Ltd., 30 York Road, Southend. Tel. 68697
ON THE EASTERN ESPLANADE
GLIDERDROME

Rocky Marciano wins the
World heavyweight title
from Jersey Joe Walcott.

**Oxford win the
Boat Race in
blizzard conditions.**

It's the smallest crowd in living
memory on Putney towpath and
conditions are the worst in
almost 70 years. Both coxes are
wearing goggles to keep out the
blinding snow.

Cambridge won the toss and
are confident of winning; only
two of last year's 'Wonder Crew'
are rowing today.

Despite the awful conditions
the race was neck and neck for
most of the course and just
about visible through the
blizzard from the spectators'
point of view. Both crews were
dead level up to the last few
strokes but Oxford managed
just to pull ahead to win by ten
feet - one sixth of a length. A
well-earned victory and a very
gallant performance by two
enthusiastic crews.

1952

Interesting Facts

A crowd eagerly wait to try out the new 'Zoomerang', a streamlined version
of the Boomerang.

**The driver of a bus
which killed 23 military
cadets is fined £20 and
loses his licence for
three years.**

**Anne Frank's diary
is published.**

Interesting Facts

The news that came from the Pathe cameras captured history in
motion. The lives of Britions were influenced by Pathe's pictorials
which delivered news of major world issues to the average British
family. Even the somewhat trivial, bizarre and intriguing events that
took place were recorded by Pathe and a selection of these interesting
facts is shown on the following pages.

**South African scientists
announce the discovery
of the Coelacanth,
a fish believed extinct
since prehistoric times.**

**Gold reserves rise
£11,000,000 in one month.**

**After 2,000 hormone
injections in Copenhagen,
George becomes
Christine Jorgenson, the
tall blonde from New
York. She was the first to
make public her sex
change and was paid
£30,000 by 'American
Weekly'.**

**Braille is re-interred
in France's
Tomb of the Great.**

**Beppo the Clown cycles
from Stafford to London
on a bicycle made from
a bedstead.**

**Zebra crossing
debate rages.**

**Sea freezes at
Whitby, Yorks.**

The minesweeper, HMS Wave, is swept on to the rocky foreshore at St. Ives, Cornwall, and badly holed. Repairs are made hurriedly and soon the ship is afloat again.

USA - 35 million TV viewers watch the most powerful atomic explosion.

Concern grows over the influence of TV on the nation.

Drought in Australia kills 80% of cattle.

Highly-skilled
aircraft workers
lured abroad by
higher wages.

George Raft, smooth
American leading
man of the 30s and
40s is allegedly
involved in dealings
with the Mafia. He
starred in 'Scarface',
'Night After Night',
'If I had a Million'
and many others.

BOAC airliner crashes
in the Sahara Desert -
many survivors.

Comet airliner crash
lands at Rome Airport.

RAF pilots scramble
to Meteor jets during
exercise 'Ardent',
Britain's largest air
defence exercise
since the Battle
of Britain.

Peers, robes and coronets cleaned in preparation for the Coronation.

31st May

The Queen Mother becomes the first woman to pilot a jet aircraft when she takes control of 'Comet'.

The Queen gives her permission to have the Coronation televised.

At the Royal Mint in London, machines are already at work to make coins bearing the head of Her Majesty and the date 1953, for distribution in Coronation Year.

The design for the new coins is the work of seventy-one-year-old Mrs Mary Gillick, who spent six months designing the image of the Queen, with the assistance of the Duke of Edinburgh.

21st April
The Queen's Birthday

Handsome Coronation souvenir pencils are being turned out by the thousands at a factory in London. Every child over five years of age, at school in London, will be given one by the London County Council next June. That means that about 432,000 pencils have to be made. Cutting, drilling, polishing - the makers are hard at it to get them ready in time.

Five million separate pieces are needed to make all the pencils. Spare leads, a blue plastic body, rolled gold bands and gold-plated clips, will make them worthy souvenirs of the great occasion.

A chef makes icing sugar crown jewels.

The Queen at the Trooping of the Colour.

The Queen opens her first Parliament.

Pathe's continual reports brought the year's major world events to its viewers and in its distinctive style also provided further pictorial news on a large variety of events ranging from lifestyle in Britain to amusing and interesting facts.

As the memorable year of 1952 ended, another began. In January, 1953 Britons witnessed the hanging of Derek Bentley at Wandsworth Prison after a plea from 200 MPs for his pardon was rejected.

In Kenya, the Mau Mau uprising had caused panic among white civilians as it gained momentum. Four months later, African rights leader Jomo Kenyatta, together with five other collaborators, was sentenced to seven years, in jail for managing the Mau Mau terrorist society.

Britain was faced with yet another death in the monarchy with the passing of Queen Mary and later in the year there was grave concern for the Prime Minister as he suffered from a serious stroke.

By June, the United States showed the world that it was leading the way in atomic technology with the detonation of the greatest ever atomic explosion so far, in Nevada, having twice the power of the Hiroshima bomb. To the suprise of the UN, the Soviet Union announced two months later that it had broken its monopoly of the hydrogen bomb.

The end to the war in Korea was received enthusiastically toward the end of the year, after three years of bloody fighting and the loss of more than two million lives.

In Britain, the year produced no end to food rationing. The Government announced its plans for commercial television which was followed by news from the Tories proclaiming the successful fullfilment of their election pledge to provide 300,000 extra homes before the year's end.

ACKNOWLEDGEMENT

The idea to produce the **Year to Remember** books was born out of the successful **Year to Remember** videos which cover the years 1930-1969.

The British Pathe News library contains some 50 million feet of film dating back to the 1890s. And as such there are probably over 200 million stills of history which could be taken from the film.

Playing stills photographer with movie film is a wonderful task. My thanks go to Ron Saunders of British Pathe News whose knowledge of the library and events is unsurpassable. Special thanks also to the staff of Dennis Fairey and Associates who designed the book. Special mention to Jane Feiven, Jackie Thorn and Sylvia Leigh for their time and effort and enthusiasm.

Ninety percent of the photographs are taken from the Pathe Film Library and were printed by the Pinewood Stills Department. Inevitably some events which needed to be included were not covered by Pathe - so the following acknowledgements are:

The Design Museum
p.62(BL), p.64(TR), p.76(BL), p.85.

Topham Picture Library
p.78, p.79, p.81, p.83, p.99, p.100, p.102, p.103, p.106, p.108.